THE HOLY LAND

A PICTURE BOOK TO REMEMBER HER BY

Designed by
DAVID GIBBON

Produced by
TED SMART

COLOUR LIBRARY INTERNATIONAL

INTRODUCTION

The Holy Land has always exerted a fascination for people from almost every part of the world. It is, of course, a land like any other, but made holy by its associations with three of the world's great religions, those of Judaism, Christianity and Islam. Over the centuries, the borders of what we term the Holy Land have changed drastically and the names by which it has been designated have also differed. It has been the 'Promised Land' of God's chosen people, the Land of Canaan, the Land of the Ammonites, of Israel and Palestine – usually at the wishes of the people who occupied the country at any particular time in history.

Geographically, the Holy Land occupies an area that extends from west to east between the Mediterranean and the Arabian Desert and from the Lebanon in the north, to the Sinai Desert in the south. The special feature of the country is the huge depression which runs from north to south and forms a valley which, for its depth, is unique in the world. This depression is marked by the River Jordan, the Dead Sea and the Wadi Arabah. Much of the Holy Land is mountainous. A large plateau, which forms the central spine, drops abruptly on one side to the Jordan and on the other side descends only gradually as it makes its way through undulating terrain towards the sea. At the northern end of the country the coastal plain is very narrow and, in fact, disappears completely as the outspurs of the Lebanon range reach the sea where, in ancient times, a passage was cut through the rock – the famous Ladder of Tyre. Towards Mount Carmel the plain widens and south of Carmel it continues to expand until, by the time it reaches Gaza it is over twelve miles wide. This area was once known as the Plain of Sharon and even in Biblical times it was noted for its fertility. The plain south of Jaffa – the present-day Tel Aviv – was formerly the land of the Philistines. The northern part of the country, around Galilee, is mountainous and south of the plain of Esdraelon are the highlands of Samaria and Judea.

Because of the geographical configuration there are notable differences in climate in various parts of the country, from the temperate heights of the plateau and the typical Mediterranean weather of the coastal region to the torrid, sweltering heat of the Ghor.

The soil of the Holy Land has been, at various times, either uncultivated and unattended or intensely farmed. It has, however, always been fertile, requiring only tilling and watering to produce abundant crops.

The jewel of the Holy Land is, of course, Jerusalem. It is doubtful if any other place on earth can have been more revered, reviled, destroyed, rebuilt and built over than Jerusalem but, despite this, its magic still comes through to captivate new generations.

Solomon's Temple was built here on Mount Moriah, at the express command of his father David, over the rock upon which it is believed Abraham was prepared to sacrifice his son Isaac, making the site the holiest of holies to all Judaism. According to the Muslim faith it was from the same rock that the prophet Mohammed began his celestial journey and it was also here, of course, that the scenes were enacted that would prove to be the foundation of Christianity. The remarkable thing is that these events and all the many others that are associated with them should all have taken place here, in an unremarkable and obscure setting in the wilderness, where no rivers meet and where there is no port to make the growth of a city likely. It seems that from its inception Jerusalem was intended as the embodiment of an ideal, a sacred rallying point to unite the tribes of Israel and, in spite of all the wrongs that human beings have been able to accomplish through the centuries, often in the name of the ideals they represented, it is still as an ideal that it exists today.

The city of Jerusalem is built on two elongated hills. It stands 750 metres above sea level and 1,150 metres above the level of the nearby Dead Sea. Divisions within the city are strictly according to faith; the Christian Quarter is situated in the north-west, the Muslim Quarter in the north-east, the Jewish Quarter in the south-east and the Armenian Quarter in the south-west.

Contained within the present city walls are: the Temple Area (which occupies about one sixth of the area of the Old City) and on which stand the beautiful Dome of the Rock and the El Aqsa Mosque, and the collection of buildings known as the Church of the Holy Sepulchre. So built over, divided, added to and re-allocated is this particular monument that it is unwise to enter it with any expectation of understanding without first consulting a good guide book. The reason for its conglomerate nature is that it is many churches now formed into one and it covers the area of Calvary, taking in the actual hill, as well as the nearby Holy Sepulchre. The problem that is unique to this particular church is that custody of and responsibility for it are shared by no less than six differing Christian sects: Roman Catholics, Greek Orthodox, Syrians, Armenians, Abyssinians and Copts, and rivalries going back many centuries continue to create almost insoluble problems.

Just outside the city walls, at the foot of the Mount of Olives, stands what is considered by many people to be one of the world's most beautiful churches – the Gethsemane Church of All Nations – built on the traditional site of the Garden of Gethsemane.

No more than half an hour's drive from Jerusalem lies the town of Bethlehem with, as its focal point, the ancient Church of the Nativity.

The Holy Land will, obviously, mean different things to different people but it would be very hard to find another area in the world that could arouse more emotion or be filled with greater interest.

David's Citadel and the Tower of David *left*

Donkeys *left* are still much in evidence in many parts of the Holy Land and the small size and almost fragile appearance of these attractive animals is belied by the heavy loads, often including a rider, that they are required to carry.

The Citadel of the Cross in Caesarea is shown *right*. This ancient city and seaport lies some 22 miles from Haifa. It was founded by Herod the Great in 13BC. In 638AD it was occupied by the Muslims, after which its importance as a port declined.

Acre *below* is a town stretching out on a promontory, at the end of which is the outer harbour enclosed by its walls, and retaining much of its Oriental appearance. The town was first mentioned in the tablets of Tell Marna under the name Acca. At one time its importance as a port was considerable but it was eventually superseded by Haifa.

The largest city and the chief commercial centre of Israel is Tel Aviv *overleaf.*

Bethlehem, in the course of any Christian visit to the Holy Land, is an obvious and logical place in which to start, for it was here that the story of Christianity began.

Bethlehem stands on a prominent rocky height only a few miles from Jerusalem. At its centre is the Church of the Nativity, built over the believed site of the grotto in which the infant Jesus was born. A basilica was built over the grotto in 330AD which has, over the years, been restored and added to. The paved square in front of the basilica occupies a part of the area of the former atrium and entry to the vestibule, which was once gained through three great doors, now has to be made through a small opening in one of them—the other two having been walled up. The flight of steps, one on either side of the great choir, lead to the grotto *left* which lies beneath the Altar of the Nativity.

The highly decorative interior of St. Catherine's Monastery is pictured *overleaf.*

Capernaum *above* is an ancient town on the shores of the Sea of Galilee and it is traditionally one of the places where Jesus is said to have taught. The remains of a synagogue of the 2nd century AD were discovered here at the beginning of this century.

Carrying their water jars on their heads in the time-honoured way of the desert, two Bedouin women are pictured *left*.

The Sandarion Monastery *right* is near Jericho, the first Canaanite city to be captured by the Israelites. Jericho was the winter residence of Herod the Great, and it was here that he died.

Above right is pictured Masada Rock and *overleaf* is shown Nazareth, pictured from a hill overlooking the town. Featured in the centre of the picture—and indeed the focal point of Nazareth, is the church built over the traditional site of the annunciation.

Nazareth has no real history predating the Christian era but it has since become known to many millions of people throughout the world as the place of the annunciation. From the basilica *left* entry may be gained to the highly venerated Grotto of the Annunciation.

At the foot of Mount Carmel lies Haifa *left*, Israel's chief port and an important manufacturing centre.

A pleasure craft, so different from the fishing boats of the bible, sails on the Sea of Galilee *above*.

The Greek Orthodox church in Nazareth is pictured *top right* and *right* is shown, tucked into the green slopes of a hill in Galilee, a Crusader castle.

The most imposing building in Jerusalem, and one of the world's most impressive religious structures, is the beautiful Dome of the Rock *left*, built on the summit of Mount Moriah, over the traditional site of the holocaust altar of the tribes of Israel.

As Bethlehem is the centre of the religious processions and ceremonies at Christmastime, so Jerusalem becomes the focal point at Easter, when the various denominations of the Christian faith process along the Via Dolorosa—the Way of Sorrows—which leads to Calvary and the Holy Sepulchre. Many thousands of people line the streets at this time and some of them may well have travelled thousands of miles to share in the moving ceremonies that are enacted in their original locations.

The Dome of the Rock is seen *overleaf* behind the old city walls of Jerusalem.

The path leading from the foot of the Mount of Olives to the summit passes behind the Gethsemane Church of All Nations *right* and up, beyond the cupolas of the Russian church of Mary Magdalene. It is a steep twisting path and climbing it can be hot and tiring. Affording a welcome respite is the church of Dominus Flevit–The Lord Wept– where tradition tells us that Jesus wept over the city of Jerusalem. From the gardens *left* the city may be seen, shimmering in the hot sun. Stepping into the cool of the church itself provides a unique sight; Jerusalem seen across the altar and framed by the wrought-iron window *below* of the church. In the gardens of the church was discovered, in 1953, a necropolis of the Jewish and Byzantine period and it is possible to see some of the tombs and sarcophagi.

At the foot of the Mount of Olives stands the Gethsemane Church of All Nations *right* with its beautiful facade and statues of the four Evangelists.

The small and almost insignificant entrance *left* over which a mass of bouganvillea blossom cascades, is in marked contrast to the imposing and beautiful facade of the Gethsemane Church of All Nations–shown in more detail on the previous page. Outside the door the souvenir sellers wait with their offers, to the many visitors who come to the garden and church every day, of colour slides, film, postcards, trinkets and, of course, objects made, so the vendors always insist, of wood from the olive trees on the Mount of Olives, or even from the Garden of Gethsemane! If all the vendors of such objects were to be believed, then the Mount of Olives would be a barren place indeed, with not a tree to be seen! In fact, the contents of the garden, the flowers, the trees and, most of all the stones from the olives, are jealously guarded by the Fransiscans. They collect the olive stones and fashion them into rosaries, both for their own use and, occasionally, to be presented to visitors. Beyond the entrance lies the garden and through the garden a side door leads into the church itself.

It has been suggested that the olive trees in the Garden of Gethsemane *right* may be over two thousand years old. It is also understood, however, that all the trees in and around Jerusalem were felled by the soldiers of Titus in 70AD to be used in the building of his war machines. It would seem unlikely, therefore, that only these particular olive trees were spared. But it must also be said that, according to Pliny, "The olive tree never dies," and it may be that the present trees, even if not the contemporaries of Jesus, are shoots from the trees that existed at that time. Whatever the truth of their age, the trees are certainly very ancient and the Garden of Gethsemane–and its trees–hold a very special place in the hearts of most Christians.

From the earliest days of the Christian Church the site of the agony in the garden was greatly revered and, in the 4th century–in the time of Theodosius–a basilica was erected there. It was subsequently destroyed by the Persians, rebuilt by the Crusaders and then destroyed yet again. The site was excavated in 1891 and plans were made to erect a new church. The present basilica *above* was finished by the Franciscans in 1924 and, as many different peoples throughout the world had helped to finance its building, the coats of arms of the United States, Canada, Germany, Great Britain, Belgium, Spain, France, Italy, Chile, Mexico, Brazil, Argentina, Poland, Eire, Hungary and Australia are all incorporated in the mosaics and the iron grill; hence the name–Church of All Nations.

Alabaster windows, which are translucent, allow a dim, purple light to filter through and illuminate the interior in the most restful way–entirely in keeping with the purpose of the church. Six columns support the twelve cupolas which form the body of the church and this gives the impression of prostration before the rock of the Agony which rises through the floor.

Above and to the right of the Church of All Nations is the beautiful and distinctive Russian church of Mary Magdalene, built in 1888 by Czar Alexander III in memory of his mother, the Empress Maria Alexandrovna. In the grounds of the Russian church are the remains of the ancient road that led to the summit of the Mount of Olives.

When we think of Jerusalem we instinctively connect it, in our minds, with its place in the history of three of the world's great religions and, of course, this is understandable. It would be wrong, however, to assume that this is all there is to Jerusalem; that it is merely a museum or a religious centre and nothing more. Jerusalem, both without and within the city walls, is a lively, bustling city. Within the old city there are certainly no department stores or large shops but it is, nevertheless, a very alive and vital place. Quite apart from the many visitors from all over the world, the parties of tourists being conducted from or to this or that place of interest, the narrow streets are thronged with people going about their business; housewives buying provisions for their families, deliveries being made–often by donkey–and Arabs from outlying areas selling their small amount of home-grown produce by the roadside. The souvenir shops, of course, are everywhere; it is difficult to walk more than a few yards down any of the streets without coming across yet another. As with most cities where tourism plays a large part in the economy there is good and bad to be found; shops that sell cheap, tasteless rubbish and others that have exquisite workmanship on show. There are 'guides' who will extract the most they can from gullible tourists and show them around the holy places with a complete disregard for the truth, and

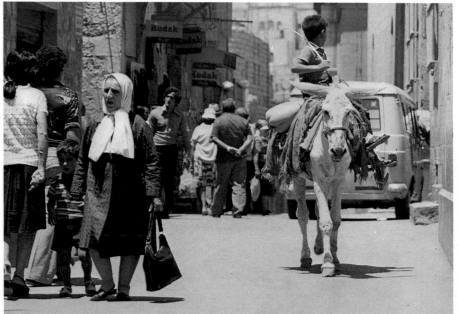

there are others who are knowledge-able, courteous and fair.

The great majority of the streets in the old city are far too narrow and crowded to allow the entry of motor vehicles and, as the city is built on two hills, the streets are often steep and, indeed, stepped. The ability and apparent willingness of donkeys to carry such a heavy burden, plus a rider, is a source of amazement to many visitiors to Jerusalem. Donkeys are to be seen everywhere, carrying anything from rubble, where building is in progress, to containers of kerosene or milk. When donkeys are not being used porters carry enormous loads on their backs or, like the one below, use peculiar three-wheeled barrows, reminiscent of the old ice cream carts, which, particularly when in the charge of the youngsters, arc often to be seen hurtling down hills with their 'drivers' sliding along behind them in a desperate and for the most part successful effort to control them.

It is difficult to imagine a building more beautiful than the Dome of the Rock, pictured on these and the following pages. It stands on the summit of Mount Moriah–so called in memory of Abraham's sacrifice. A temple was originally built by Solomon on the site but it was not until the 7th century that it started to take anything like its present form. Successively restored, it achieved the height of its magnificence under Suleiman the Magnificent in the 16th century, and it was at this time that the outer part was covered with coloured tiles, details of which are shown overleaf.

Under the Dome, and surrounded by the iron screen of the Crusaders, lies the rock, made sacred by history and legend. Here Abraham was prepared to sacrifice his son Isaac and it was this rock that became the foundation of the holocaust altar. According to the Muslims, Mohammed came to Jerusalem and prayed on the rock before continuing his journey to heaven on his magnificent steed Burak, a gift from the Archangel Gabriel.

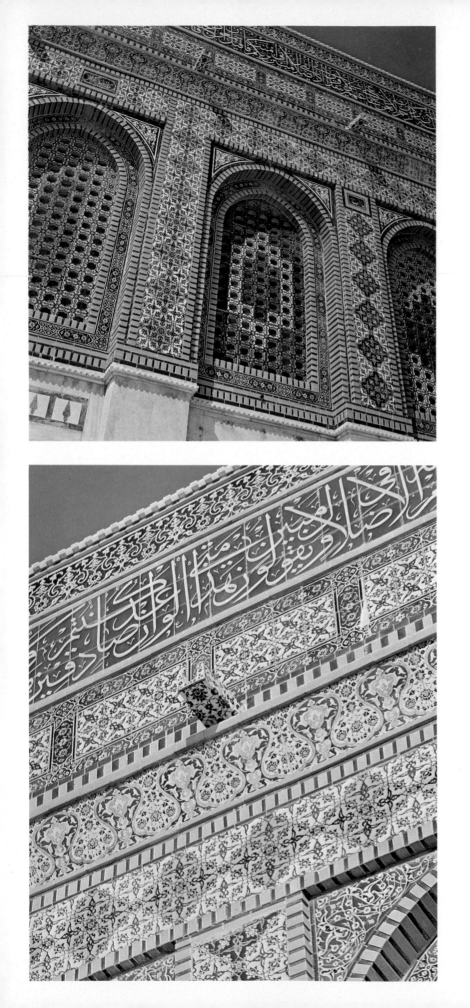

In the time of Herod the Great a magnificent Temple was built on the site of the old; on the summit of Mount Moriah. All that remains of this building, apart from the Rock itself, is the western, or wailing wall. Following the Arab conquest of Jerusalem in 638AD a building was erected over the Rock but the Dome of the Rock as we know it was not completed until 691.

Mohammed did not see himself as a Messiah but, rather, as the last of the great line of prophets, many of whom are common to the Koran and the Old and New Testaments. Abraham, therefore, occupies a place of importance to the Muslims that corresponds to that afforded him by the Jews–and, indeed, the Christians. Because of this the Rock on Mount Moriah has a special significance to the followers of Mohammed, not only as Abraham's sacrificial altar, but also as the place made holy by the Prophet when he stopped to pray there on his journey to visit the other prophets in heaven. According to the religion of Islam the Rock is the foundation stone of the world, exceeded in holiness only by the Kaaba stone in Mecca.

The first Muslim construction over the Rock was a wooden mosque, but this was only a temporary expedient, to be superseded by the Dome of the Rock proper, which was built between 687 and 791 by the Caliph Abd al-Malik, who used for the purpose a great number of Roman pillars and stones as well as employing architects and designers local to the area. The use of pillars from other buildings accounts for the difference in styles that are apparent today.

In 1099 the Crusaders transformed the mosque into a Christian sanctuary, giving it the name *Templum Domini* and handed it over to the custody of a Chapter of the Canons of St. Augustine. This was not to last for long, however, and in 1187, when Jerusalem was recaptured by Saladin, the golden cross on the top of the dome was removed–to be replaced by the Crescent of Islam.

Framed between two massive pillars stands the Dome of the Rock *above* in splendid isolation on the summit of Mount Moriah. The pillars support arches, called *Mawazin*– which means 'scales'–by the Muslims, as they believe that from these arches scales will be suspended, to be used in the weighing of souls on the day of judgement.

The exquisite building, a perfect octagon, is crowned by the dome, sheathed in gold-plated aluminium. Although this may not match the richness of the original dome, which legend tells us was covered with solid gold, the present structure at least matches the original in appearance, and is a vast improvement on the dull, lead dome that was erected in the 11th century.

After the narrow, crowded and sometimes evil-smelling streets of the old city, the vast, open space in which the Dome of the Rock stands is almost like a breath of fresh air, and the very contrast makes the peace and quiet of this holy place seem even more unreal.

A niche in the wall inside the Dome of the Rock indicates to the true follower of Mohammed the direction of Mecca, towards which he will face during his daily prayers.

Eight wide flights of steps lead up to the platform on which the Dome of the Rock stands—and which is the summit of Mount Moriah. The whole effect is one of immense spaciousness. The soaring arches *left* span elegant pillars, many of them bound with iron hoops now to add support to them because of their great age.

Fed by the waters of Solomon's aqueduct is El Kas, *below* the ablution fountain at which the Muslim faithful carry out the obligatory washing of hands, feet and head before entering the mosque to pray.

At the southern end of the esplanade stands the El Aqsa Mosque *right*—the distant mosque—so called because at the time that it was built, at the beginning of the 8th century, it was the most distant mosque from Mecca. Although it does not, perhaps, have the unique splendour of the nearby Dome of the Rock, the El Aqsa Mosque is a fascinating building in its own right. Parts of the original structure still survive to the present day as part of the extensive renovation and rebuilding that took place between 1938 and 1942.

All over Jerusalem constant excavation and reconstruction *above* is carried out and the results of this work are to be seen almost everywhere.

The Temple Area, or Haram Esh-Sharif, contains a wealth of sanctuaries, shrines and memorials, *left* the names of which have often been changed over the centuries to fit in with the ideas and beliefs of the city's many conquerors.

The interior of the El Aqsa Mosque *right* reveals an impressive open space of approximately 85 metres long by 60 metres wide. Much of the material used in its construction was taken from St. Mary's Church and this lends to the building a peculiar church-like feeling. The whole of the floor is covered with large carpet squares in a variety of patterns. The priceless pulpit, constructed in Aleppo without the use of nails, and the gift of Saladin, was sadly destroyed in 1969 by an arsonist who managed to gain entry to the mosque with a can of kerosene, with the result that an irreplaceable work of art was lost to the world.

Small boys selling their wares from a bench in the old city *above* are suddenly aware of the camera and unsure whether they want to be photographed or not.

Two time-honoured methods of carrying loads. A heavily laden donkey *left* and two equally heavily laden women *right* and always in evidence, the ubiquitous plastic shopping bag.

It is possible to buy an enormous variety of goods in the old city, from exotic souvenirs to simple, everyday fresh fruit and vegetables *below*.

It is difficult to imagine that the assortment of towers and cupolas *overleaf* in reality mark the site of a hill and a garden tomb, but such is the case with the Church of the Holy Sepulchre.

A small arched doorway *left* provides access to the courtyard *right* of the group of chapels, churches and monasteries that, together, make up the Church of the Holy Sepulchre. The door at the right has been bricked up since the time of Saladin.

From the inside of the church, looking towards the main entrance *below*. The Stone of the Anointing is at the bottom left of the picture, surrounded by eight candelabra.

The Roman Catholic altar *far right top* on the summit of the rock of Calvary, dates from the latter part of the 16th century.

The Church of the Holy Sepulchre takes its name from the tomb *far right bottom* where the body of Jesus was laid after the crucifixion. Most of the rock from which the tomb was carved has been cut away and what remains has been richly panelled, pillared and decorated *bottom right* by the various Christian sects into whose care it is entrusted.

Bethlehem, the birthplace of King David and of Jesus, lies about eleven miles south of Jerusalem. The present Church of the Nativity dates from the 6th century and, because the Magi were depicted as Persians in the mosaics, it is said to be the only church they spared when they overran the country in 614AD.

Christmas bells *left* still hung with coloured electric lights, above the Church of the Nativity.

The main entrance to the Church of the Nativity *below* has a doorway so small that it is necessary to bend almost double to gain access.

The focal point of the church in Bethlehem is the silver star *right* which marks the place of the Nativity. This particular star dates from 1717 and the Latin inscription around it reads– Hic de Virgine Maria Jesus Christus natus est'– (Here was Jesus Christ born of the Virgin Mary).

MILITARY COMMAND
JUDAEA AND SAMARIA
MINISTRY OF RELIGIOUS AFFAIRS
RULES FOR VISITORS

1. THE PLACE WHICH YOU ARE VISITING IS HOLY.
2. PLEASE CONDUCT YOURSELF WITH DUE RESPECT FOR IT.
3. SMOKING IS PROHIBITED.
4. CLEANLINESS SHOULD BE STRICTLY KEPT.
5. ABSOLUTE SILENCE IS URGED.
6. MODEST DRESS DEMEANOUR IS ESSENTIAL.
7. EATING AND DRINKING WITHIN THESE PRECINCTS ARE ABSOLUTELY FORBIDDEN.
8. NO CHURCH PROPERTY MAY BE TOUCHED.
9. NO HEAD-DRESS MAY BE WORN WITHIN THE PRECINCTS.
10. THE BRINGING IN OF ANIMALS IS PROHIBITED.
11. ARMS MAY NOT BE TAKEN WITHIN THE CHURCH.
12. PHOTOGRAPHS MAY BE TAKEN BUT NO OF MEMBERS OF THE CLERGY.

VISITORS MUST ADHERE TO ANY INSTRUCTIONS GIVEN BY RESPONSIBLE STAFF AND GUARDIANS OF THE CHURCH OFFENDERS WILL BE PUNISHED

מפקדת
אזור יהודה והשומרון
משרד הדתות
הוראות למבקרים

1. המקום אשר אתה מבקר קדוש הוא.
2. יש להתנהג ביראת כבוד במקום.
3. אסור לעשן.
4. יש להקפיד על שמירת הנקיון.
5. יש להקפיד על שקט מוחלט.
6. יש להקפיד על צניעות הלבוש וההנהגה הנאותה.
7. האכילה והשתיה אסורות בהחלט.
8. אין לגעת ברכוש הכנסיה.
9. הכניסה למקום הינה בגלוי ראש.
10. הכנסת בעלי חיים אסורה.
11. הכניסה עם נשק אסורה.
12. תצלום מותר פרט לצלום אנשי כמורה.

על המבקרים לציית להוראות האחראים השומרים במקום העברינים ייענשו כחוק

David's Citadel and the Tower of David *above and left* stand close to the Jaffa Gate and form part of the west wall of the city. A great deal of archaeological excavation is being carried out here, particularly at the base of the massive city walls.

The monument known as Absalom's Pillar *right* in the Valley of Kidron with, beyond it, the east wall of the city, culminating in the pinnacle of the Temple at the left.

David's third son, Absalom, exploited anything that could bring about discontent in the tribes. He eventually had himself proclaimed king, and this inevitably meant that a battle was fought between the forces of David and those of Absalom. In the battle Absalom was defeated, and in attempting to escape, legend has it that his long hair caught in the low branches of a tree, from which he was suspended helplessly until the arrival of David's forces, who killed him.

Although the pillar commemorates Absalom it is distinctly Hellenic in style and it was probably the tomb of a wealthy Greek family.

The Israel Museum complex, with the coolly welcoming sound of its waterfalls and the landscaped beauty of its sculpture gardens, provides a fitting showcase for a large number of treasured and fascinating exhibits. High on the list of anyone interested in a study of the Holy Land must be the Dead Sea Scrolls, housed in the Shrine of the Book, *right*, designed to represent, from the outside, the lid of one of the earthenware jars in which the scrolls were discovered, in a remote cave by the Dead Sea.

South from the Jaffa Gate lies Yemin Moshe. A settlement dating from the latter half of the nineteenth century, it was the result of a dream of a new Jerusalem outside the walls of the old city. Standing somewhat incongruously atop the old settlement and dwarfed, now, by the encroaching high rise blocks stands the Montefiore Windmill, *left*, named after Sir Moses Montefiore whose vision and idealism brought about the building of Yemin Moshe which was to lead, eventually, to the construction of the modern Jerusalem we see today.

Sightless eyes and a grotesquely twisted nose in the side of a hillock opposite the Damascus Gate bear an uncanny resemblance to a skull, *left*. The site excited General Gordon of Khartoum, a devout Christian, sufficiently for him to make an exhaustive search of the adjacent area. The eventual discovery, nearby, of an ancient oil press and a tomb cut out of the solid rock convinced him that he had found the true site of Calvary, or Golgotha–the place of the skull. Authentic or not, the whole site is now preserved, with its relics, in the form of a very beautiful and peaceful garden which certainly gives some idea of how the area now covered by the Church of the Holy Sepulchre must have looked two thousand years ago.

Grouped amongst trees, a short distance west of the old city, stand the Convention Centre, the Hebrew University, the Planetarium, the Stadium and the Israel Museum, from which may be seen the uncompromising squareness of the Knesset, *right*, Israel's new Parliament building with its superb Chagall hall.

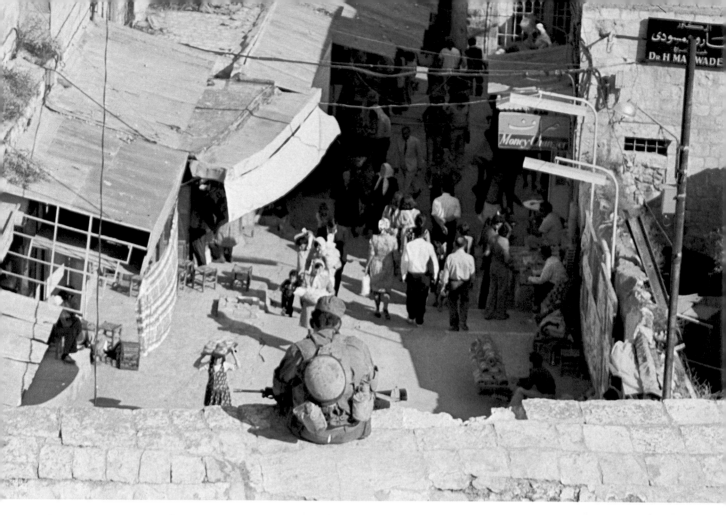

An Israeli soldier *left* sits on the wall directly above the busy Damascus Gate, one of the main entrances into the old city, keeping a watchful eye on the comings and goings below him. The walls and the city's narrow, twisting streets are regularly patrolled by troops, but the city has seen it all before; it seems that there have always been troops of one power or another in Jerusalem throughout its long and troubled history.

Most of the streets in the old city are very narrow *below, far left* and, with the awnings over the shops and stalls–or the buildings themselves– almost meeting overhead, only a narrow band of sunlight is allowed to filter through and illuminate the cobbles.

A small boy, probably unaware that he is surrounded by so much history sees only an inquisitive photographer and, equally inquisitive himself, obliges him with a backwards glance.

Carrying his wares strapped firmly on his back and around his waist, a tea vendor *above* dispenses hot, sweet tea to passers by. On a hot, dry day there are few drinks more refreshing than his. The decorated and polished urn on his back contains the tea and the spout sticks out from under his left arm. In his left hand he carries a heavy brass water container to rinse out the glasses before they are returned to the tray at his waist.

Traders and craftsmen are to be found by the roadside throughout the streets of the old city. Some are relatively well equipped and others may only have an old box containing a few apples or some pieces of material and it is difficult to see how some of them manage to make any sort of living at all. Others, like the shoe seller pictured here *left* supplement their few sales by carrying out minor repairs with only the very minimum of equipment.

The colour and excitement of a ceremony at the wailing wall *overleaf* as relatives and friends shout encouragement and record the scene for family albums.

The earliest records refer to Jerusalem as Salem and, later, Urusalem –certainly one of the most important cities of Palestine–although subject to the power of Egypt. When David eventually took the city a palace was built on Mount Zion and defences were erected around the city.

When David was growing old, he had his son Solomon anointed king. At the same time he commanded Solomon to build a Temple on Mount Moriah, something David had been unable to accomplish in his own lifetime because he had been too occupied in wars and establishing the kingdom. After David died, Solomon approached Hiram, the king of Tyre, and asked him to build the Temple. Cedars were brought from the Lebanon to the port of Jaffa and then overland to by used in the Temple's construction. The top of Mount Moriah, where Abraham had prepared to sacrifice his son Isaac, was levelled and on it was built the Temple, together with a royal palace and a mound to connect the new buildings with the city of David, and around it all he built a wall, known as the first wall.

In the 6th century BC Nebuchadnezzar laid siege to the city, destroyed the Temple and led the people away into captivity. Under the edict of Cyrus the Jews were permitted to return to Jerusalem, and they did so, restoring the altar and the Temple, but this state of affairs only lasted until the domination of Israel by Persia, followed by the conquest by Alexander the Great in 331BC. After the break-up of Alexander's empire Jerusalem passed into the hands of the Ptolemies of Egypt, and later the Seleucids of Syria. The tyranny of Antiochus was directly responsible for the rise of the Maccabees, a rise to power that restored some of the greatness that had been Jerusalem's during the reign of Solomon. Once again, however, the problem of internal discord arose in the city and, this time, it led to the intervention of the greatest power the world had known; the power of Rome. Pompey made himself master of Jerusalem in 63BC and in 37BC the Romans installed Herod as king; an act that was to have far-reaching consequences so far as the Jerusalem we know today is concerned.

The many magnificent buildings that were commenced during the reign of Herod the Great were, alas, destroyed by the soldiers of Titus in 70AD. There was one notable exception, however, and that was the western wall of Herod's Temple, which was left virtually intact. It is believed that this was done deliberately to show the world the might of Rome and to act as an object lesson to all; to show that even buildings of a magnitude such as this had fallen before Rome's power. It is this wall that is the subject of these pages; a wall constructed of huge limestone blocks and which reaches a height of almost sixty feet, dwarfing the figures of the people who come here to pray.

After the destruction of the old city of Jerusalem by Titus in 70AD the Romans built on the site a new city, Aelia Capitolina, in 135AD. The Jews were not allowed to enter the new city but they were permitted to weep on the sacred rock that had been the holocaust altar of their Temple.

When Jerusalem fell to the Arabs the rock was covered by the Dome of the Rock and so even this holy place was denied to the Jews. They had to be content with coming to the wall, the only remaining part of their original Temple and there they sorrowed, not least for all that had been and was now no more.

There have been attempts in the past to build a synagogue at the wall and in 1929 this idea caused a great deal of trouble. Eventually, after an International Commission, the idea was abandoned. Today there are other plans, one of which is to excavate the wall to an even lower level, to go even further back in history to a time nearer to the origins of the Temple, and impressions of some of these ideas are on view in the musuem by the Jaffa Gate.

Whatever may happen in the future, the wall is a place of the utmost sanctity to Jews from all over the world, many thousands of whom travel great distances to visit and pray at this venerable place. At sunset each day, but particularly on holy days, Jews arrive from all parts of the city and, indeed, from much further afield to offer their prayers and, sometimes, to push written requests into the spaces between the great stones, there, they hope, to find a more direct route to God.

Some idea of the part of the wall that is at present above the ground may be gained from this view *above.* At the wall the men are segregated from the women by a fence. Beyond and above the wall rises the huge dome of the Dome of the Rock, under which is the sacred holocaust altar of Solomon's Temple.

On the summit of the Mount of Olives stands the now rather forlorn-looking Chapel of the Ascension *above*. A Crusaders reconstruction, it stands on the site of the original church built in 378AD. In 1187 the place was converted into a mosque and the arcades of the edicule were walled up.

Stones on the tombs in the Jewish cemetery *left* are left by visitors to commemorate their attendance. The sinking sun brilliantly backlights the Dome of the Rock in the middle distance and some of the newer towers on the skyline.

First published in Great Britain 1978 by Colour Library International Ltd.
© Illustrations: Colour Library International Ltd. Colour separations by La Cromolito, Milan, Italy.
Display and text filmsetting by Focus Photoset, London, England.
Printed and bound by L.E.G.O. Vicenza, Italy.
All rights reserved. ISBN No. 0 904681 75 0
COLOUR LIBRARY INTERNATIONAL